Feeling Afraid

by Rochelle Nielsen Barsuhn
illustrated by
Gwen Connelly

ELGIN, ILLINOIS 60120

Distributed by Childrens Press, 1224 West Van Buren Street, Chicago, Illinois 60607.

Library of Congress Cataloging in Publication Data

Barsuhn, Rochelle Nielsen, 1958-
  Feeling afraid.

  (What's in a word?)
  Rev. ed. of: Afraid. ©1982.
  Summary: A small child discovers that there are
many things to fear, such as storms, making friends,
being laughed at, and confessing to misdeeds.
    1. Fear—Juvenile literature. [1. Fear.
2. Emotions] I. Connelly, Gwen, ill. II. Title.
BF575.F2B345 1982b   152.4   82-19946
ISBN 0-89565-246-3

1 2 3 4 5 6 7 8 9 10 11 12 R 89 88 87 86 85 84 83

Feeling Afraid

Afraid—To be filled with fear;
to be scared; to think something
bad is going to happen.

Sometimes
new things
frighten me.
I want to stay home
where I'm safe.

But I'm sailing off into today,
as captain of my own small boat.
It's fun to explore
secret places
and to go adventuring
in new worlds.

I'm careful,
after all.

Sometimes,
I AM AFRAID
when I don't need to be.

Shadows crawl on my bedroom walls,
and sounds outside my window
wake me up.

WHOOSH!
THUMP!
SCRATCH-SCRATCH-SCRATCH!

My heart beats hard,
and I wonder,
"WHAT'S THAT?!"

Then I sneak
a one-eyed peek.
It's just Midnight, the next door cat.

It rained and rained.
Thunder boomed.
The windows rattled in the panes.
I covered my ears
and crouched behind the couch.

Then Dad popped salty popcorn
for us to eat,
and we cuddled together
feeling safe and warm.

When our teacher asked,
"What's ten minus two?"
the class raised and waved hands.
"Six!" yelled Susan.
Tony said, "Seven."

I knew the answer,
but I stayed quiet as a kitten
in my seat.
"What if I'm wrong?" I thought.

But finally,
I lifted my hand (just a little).
Even when you're shaking inside,
it sometimes feels good to try.

Lana is new at school.
If I ate lunch with her,
I'd ask if she likes
balloons on strings,
bare feet,
and cattails from the creek,
like I do.

But
    I'm
        too
            shy.

Other times, being

AFRAID

helps keep me safe.

"Come home before dark,"
Mom called as I headed out
to meet Marsha at the park.

But we climbed tall trees
till the day turned dark
and crickets chirped.

It was a long way home
all alone
in the dark.

I walked fast.
The bushes shivered
as I passed.

I ran the rest of the way,
thinking of what Mom would say.

Tom's dog, Samson,
is big as a bike.
He might bite
if I pet him.
And Mom always says,
"Be careful with dogs you don't know."

But Tom hugged him.
"He's nice," he said.
"He doesn't bite."

I let Samson sniff my hand.
His tail wagged.
Then I patted his fuzzy head.
He was happy.
Now we're friends.

"Dive!" the teacher yelled.
My friends dived
one
by
one into the
       deep
          blue
            pool.

I shivered at the edge,
looking down.
My teacher said, "That's okay.
Jump here where it's not so deep."

. . . Finally, I gulped a breath,
held my nose, and
          jumped!

Next I'll try a dive.

The horses at the farm
pranced lickety-split
across the grass and back again.

I wanted to ride,
bouncing high in the saddle.
But the horses were so fast and tall,
I thought,
"I can't. I'll fall."

Uncle Harry lifted me up
on his horse's strong brown back.
He held me tightly.
We trotted around the track.

Someday, when I can,
I'll ride a horse again—
by myself.

But even when

I'M AFRAID

I should do what's right.

Karen stole Judy's lunch
and ate it, apple and all,
behind the tree.

I saw her.
I should tell my teacher.
But Karen might find out who told.

"Want to come over after school?"
Wendy asked.
"We can tell knock-knock jokes
and jump on my pogo stick."

I wanted to go,
but Wendy is tall and skinny as a pencil,
and the kids laugh at her.

Will they laugh at me, too,
if I'm her friend?

GINGERSNAPS!
I ate them all.

But when Mom asked,
"Did you eat the gingersnaps?"
I said, "No."
I was afraid to tell.
Now I'm sorry.

In the school program
I have to tell
a Christmas story
after Paul's poem.

I'm sitting here
with my eyes shut,
remembering all the words
I'm supposed to say.

I can do it
even though I'm afraid.
It's my turn.
Ready,
recite!

I did it!
I did all right.

About the Author:

Rochelle Nielsen Barsuhn studied English literature at Bethel College (St. Paul, Minnesota). Her written work has appeared in several magazines for children. Ms. Barsuhn describes herself as "a reader of books—children's, the classics, and anything in print." Currently, she works with her husband in their Minneapolis-based design and advertising agency.

About the Artist:

Gwen Connelly studied fine art at the University of Montana. After working in several areas of commercial art, Ms. Connelly now concentrates her efforts toward illustrating for children. She has illustrated several picture books, and contributed to numerous educational programs. Ms. Connelly's studio is a converted French coach house in Highland Park, Illinois, where she lives with her daughter and husband.